✠

THE PILGRIMS' WAY
FROM WINCHESTER TO CANTERBURY

Other titles in the Pilgrim Guide series

PILGRIM · GUIDE

THE PILGRIMS' WAY
FROM WINCHESTER TO CANTERBURY

Christopher Martin

Illustrated by
Jill Bentley

CANTERBURY
PRESS
Norwich

For J. H. F. B.,
with whom I first walked the Pilgrims' Way
and, fifty years later, hope to do so again.

Text © Christopher Martin 1999
Illustrations © Jill Bentley 1999

First published in 1999 by The Canterbury Press Norwich
(a publishing imprint of Hymns Ancient & Modern Limited
a registered charity)
St Mary's Works, St Mary's Plain
Norwich, Norfolk NR3 3BH

Christopher Martin has asserted his right under the Copyright, Designs
and Patents Act 1988, to be identified as Author of this work.

British Library Cataloguing in Publication Data

A catalogue record for this book is available
from the British Library

ISBN 1-85311-251-8

Typeset by Rowland Phototypesetting Ltd,
Bury St Edmunds, Suffolk
Printed and bound in Great Britain by
Redwood Books, Trowbridge, Wilts

Contents

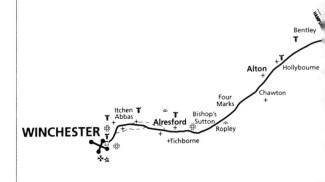

THE PILGRIMS' WAY

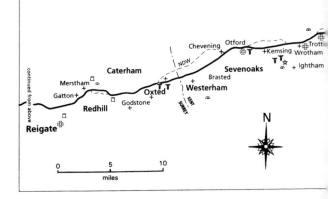

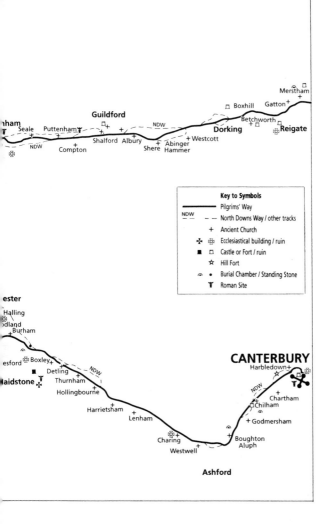

Merstham

Guildford

□ Boxhill

Gatton

Betchworth

NDW

□

Dorking

Reigate

ham

Seale

Puttenham

NDW

Shalford

Albury

Westcott

Compton

Shere

Abinger

Hammer

Key to Symbols

	Pilgrims' Way
NDW – –	North Downs Way / other tracks
+	Ancient Church
✣	Ecclesiastical building / ruin
■ □	Castle or Fort / ruin
☆	Hill Fort
⌒ •	Burial Chamber / Standing Stone
⊤	Roman Site

ester

Halling

dland

Burham

esford

Boxley

NDW

CANTERBURY

Harbledown

Detling

Maidstone

Thurnham

Hollingbourne

NDW

Chartham

Chilham

Harrietsham

Godmersham

Lenham

Charing

Boughton

Aluph

Westwell

Ashford

Introduction

The Pilgrims' Way runs from Winchester to Canterbury. It is 120 miles long and for the greater part of its length follows the line of the North Downs right across Surrey and through most of Kent. It is the route traditionally said to have been taken by the penitent King Henry II soon after the murder of Archbishop Thomas Becket at Canterbury Cathedral. Within a few years of that murder on 29 December 1170, Becket's shrine became very popular as a place of pilgrimage, as Chaucer's *Canterbury Tales* reflect. And so it remained until the Reformation under Henry VIII.

Tradition therefore imagines large numbers of pilgrims following this royal trail. It pictures them coming from the west of England, from Wales and perhaps too from Normandy, where the king had been when he heard the news of Becket's death.

This tradition lacks evidence. There is no medieval record that this was a route used by pilgrims, and such hints as can be gleaned from place-names along the way are spurious. 'The Pilgrims' Way' was first referred to on a map published by John Roche in 1752. On that map it was the name given to a stretch of track on the downs above Maidstone. The Gothic Revival was under way, and soon the name was being used all along the route that we call the Pilgrims' Way today.

A hundred years later a Victorian antiquarian named A. Way published the first definitive guide-book, and in 1895 a lady called Julia Cartwright produced one that is still in print. In 1904, a book by Hilaire Belloc entitled *The Old Road* attempted to define precisely every step of the Pilgrims' Way. That was the high-water mark of belief in the Way. By the 1920s historians were pouring scorn on the whole idea that there ever had been such a pilgrim route. By the 1950s the *Surrey Archaeological Journal* refused even to consider the possibility.

Even so, the route has remained popular, not only for long-distance walking (under its secular title, the North Downs Way) but also for Christian pilgrims. In 1988, for instance, to mark the one thousandth anniversary of the death of St Dunstan, a group drawn from churches dedicated to his name came right across the south of England from Glastonbury, where he was educated, to Canterbury, where he was archbishop. Since then the writer and broadcaster Shirley du Boulay has published *The Road to Canterbury*, an account of her journey along the Pilgrims' Way. In the year 2000, the dioceses of Winchester, Guildford, Southwark, Rochester and Canterbury are staging a year-long pilgrimage involving every parish church along the Way. All along the route today there are by-roads and properties with pilgrim connotations in their names.

Even those who are not too concerned about historical accuracy may be glad to have a few indications that the very first pilgrim to use this route may indeed have been Henry II. When news of Becket's death reached the king he was in Normandy. Very soon after hearing it, he crossed from Cherbourg to Southampton, and for the night of his arrival in England there is a record of a bill of four shillings for housing his escort of marines in Winchester. There is also record that he travelled *iter corraedio ripuit* – 'he snatched his journey in a two wheeler', and that four days later, looking suitably penitential, he arrived in Canterbury.

What is not clear is whether he went straight to Canterbury on hearing the news of Becket's murder or went some time later, after a summer season of fighting in Ireland. Conventional historians say he deferred his visit to Canterbury, but there is much to be said for thinking that he went there immediately. 'Who will rid me of this turbulent priest?' he is widely remembered as saying, but his grief and shock when he heard the news were, no doubt, heartfelt. Around midwinter he would have had time for a hasty journey to Canterbury before he set sail for Ireland. Such main roads as there were would have taken him through London, but he would not have dared to show his face in the capital at that moment. Becket's murder had further fuelled the anger of his already disgruntled subjects. So instead he might have taken the more direct route along the line of the

North Downs. Travelling thirty miles a day, he might well have spent his nights at Farnham, Reigate and Maidstone, all places that would have been able to offer him convenient lodging. Indeed, half-way along the route in Reigate we will find the strongest piece of evidence that the king did indeed pass this way, and so hallow it for generations of pilgrims to come.

There are several reasons why people go on pilgrimage. They may be looking for their roots, and if one is English a journey to Canterbury is a good way of doing this. Or they may be travelling in penitence, and what could be more appropriate than to follow in the footsteps of Henry II? Then again, a pilgrimage may be a quest for healing. In its heyday St Thomas' shrine was revered as a place where miracles happened, and it grew rich on its reputation. A pilgrimage can also be a 'beating of the bounds' to claim that a certain tract of territory in some manner belongs to us. It can also be a journey of hope. Finally, it can offer a sense of home-coming. A pilgrimage to Canterbury may fulfil any one of these purposes.

This book does not attempt to provide an exact guide for a pilgrim who is walking the route. For that purpose there is Alan Charles' admirable guidebook *Exploring the Pilgrims' Way* (Catherine Press, Newbury, 1990). Within the compass of these pages it is possible only to give a general itinerary, with various suggestions for walkers to follow. There are also some references to places of interest along the Way.

The purist may want to walk every step of the

journey, but over two stretches the route is uncertain – in east Hampshire around Alton and crossing the Medway Valley. It might be wise to use a means of transport other than 'Shanks's pony' for these stretches!

Whatever motivates any particular pilgrim, this ancient Irish blessing is appropriate for those who are setting out on this pilgrimage:

May the roads rise with you
And the wind be always at your back,
May the sun shine ever upon your face
And may the Lord hold you in the hollow of his hand.
Amen.

First Day
Winchester to Alresford
(twelve miles)

Before the pilgrim sets out for Canterbury, Winchester invites exploration. Founded by the Romans, it was the capital of King Alfred's kingdom of Wessex before London supplanted it. A fine statue of the king stands at the east end of the High Street. It was put up in 1901 to commemorate the eleven hundredth anniversary of his reign. The plaque records that the Earl of Rosebery (who had been a Liberal Prime Minister in the 1890s) made a speech at its unveiling. At that time, when the British Empire was at its height, the noble monarch was seen as the 'Founder of the kingdom and nation'.

Winchester's greatest pride is its cathedral, which, until Liverpool's Anglican Cathedral was built, claimed the longest Gothic nave in Europe (556 feet). Anyone who is new to the city should explore the lanes to the south and peep into Winchester College, founded in 1347 by William of Wykeham. To the east of the college stands the ruins of Wolvesey Palace, the medieval home of the bishops of Winchester. One of the city's most precious gems is the Hospital of St Cross, England's oldest almshouse (1137). It was the model for the almshouse in Anthony Trollope's

City Bridge, Winchester

novel *The Warden*. It used to house twenty-five poor men, and here the genuine traveller may still claim 'wayfarer's dole' – a beaker of beer and a crust of bread.

It is time to set out on the first leg of the pilgrimage. There has never been a definitive pilgrim route out of the city and pilgrims may choose from a number of well-trodden paths. Leaving the city by Hyde Street, past Hyde Abbey, one approach to the Pilgrims' Way is not difficult to find, since for the most part it follows the course of the River Itchen to the right, and is signed as 'The Itchen Way'. Another route is along St John's Street, Beggars Lane and then through Winnall Moors, with the Itchen to one's left. For the first few miles the sound of traffic on the M3 and the A34 reminds the pilgrim of the noisy present-day world. Then, as the Itchen Valley swings east, the path alongside it offers the pleasures of a country walk. By Itchen Stoke an old bridge takes the pilgrim across the river. From there the Way climbs across a golf-course and then comes back down to the river's edge. An official diversion then takes it to the breast of Alresford Hill and along the line of the new bypass to Bishops Sutton, just beyond Alresford.

It would be a good idea to drop down into the town to spend the first night there. When I first walked the Way, back in 1951, bed and breakfast at what was then the town's best hotel, 'The Swan', cost thirteen shillings and sixpence. Today a prudent pilgrim might book accommodation at Old Alresford

Old Alresford Church

Place, the Winchester Diocesan Retreat House. A former rectory, it was the home of Mary Sumner, the Victorian rector's wife who started the Mothers' Union here in 1885. A pilgrim today may be glad to end the first day's journey with the Mothers' Union prayer:

Almighty God, our heavenly Father,
who gave marriage to be a blessing,
we thank you for family life, with all its joys
and sorrows.
May we know your presence and peace in our homes
fill them with your love and use them to your glory.
Bless all who are married and every parent and child;
pour out upon us your Holy Spirit
that we may truly love and serve.
Bless the members of the Mothers' Union throughout
the world;
unite us in prayer and worship to love and serve,
that, strengthened by your grace, we may seek
to do your will,
through Jesus Christ our Lord.
Amen.

Second Day
Alresford to Alton (eleven miles)

On the second day's journey the pilgrim goes from the Itchen Valley over a ridge into the catchment of the Thames. A dedicated pilgrim may be happy to walk, but there is a seductive alternative – a steam train. Before Dr Beeching's axe, the railway line used to run from Alton to Winchester, but only the portion of it that runs eastwards from Alresford has been preserved. It is known as the Watercress Line, and to ride it would save the pilgrim the bother of clambering up to Four Marks, a somewhat sprawling place, but home to the Bishop of Basingstoke, that sits on top of the ridge.

For those who are determined to walk, there is nothing for it but to follow the A31 gently uphill through Ropley. But when the road swings to the left by an inn called The Chequers at Ropley, the pilgrim should go up a tree-lined lane that makes steady work of the slow ascent to Swelling Hill. It provides a well-earned moment to look back. Winchester is out of sight, tucked down in its valley, but the rolling landscape of hill and dale says 'Welcome to the West Country', or, to the eastbound traveller, 'Farewell'.

The descent towards Alton is mostly along lanes

Jane Austen's House, Chawton

marked by name, but where Willis Lane leads off eastwards from Hawthorn Lane, a footpath running in a north-easterly direction along the edge of a wood goes to Woodhall Farm. Below that a track goes under the embankment of the disused Meon Valley Railway, which offers steady walking in the direction of Alton.

At this point devout pilgrims may want to make a detour to visit the Anglican Benedictine monastery of Our Lady and St John, founded in 1884, and known for its manufacture of Communion wafers, which lies deep in the woods to the north of the route. Piety might expect the Pilgrims' Way to be lined with religious houses, much as motorways have their service stations, but eastwards from here and all through Surrey there is nothing, unless one departs significantly from the Way. Apart from the Stacklands retreat house on the downs above Kemsing, only the Priory of the Friars Carmelite at Aylesford makes a conscious effort to welcome pilgrims.

Rather, it is a different sort of piety that beckons as the Way heads towards Alton. For in the village of Chawton (which has at last been left in a semblance of Georgian peace, thanks to some new road diversions) lived Jane Austen, and any pilgrimage that is, at least in part, a celebration of England and Englishness should include a visit to her house. Her pictures of contemporary clergy were not flattering, and even in her 'Gothick' novel *Northanger Abbey* she did not mention the Pilgrims' Way. But she had a real

Christian faith, and she wrote a number of prayers, of which this is one:

Incline us, O God, to think humbly of ourselves,
to be serene only in the examination of our own conduct,
to consider our fellow-creatures with kindness
and to judge all that they say and do
with that charity we would desire from them ourselves.
Amen.

Third Day
Alton to Farnham (nine miles)

From Alton to Farnham the route follows the line of
the River Wey. So do the A31 and the railway, and so
it is more pleasant to walk through the villages that
have been bypassed – Holybourne, Froyle and Bentley. However, along this stretch even Hilaire Belloc,
keen as he was to establish a definitive route, had to
admit himself baffled. The route suggested is fur-
nished with a succession of footpaths, but they are not
signed or named as part of a long-distance walk. The
chief features of interest here are the Lord Mayor
Treloar School and the Lord Mayor Treloar College.

They provide an education for physically handi-
capped children and young people from all over the
country and beyond. They date back to the early
years of the twentieth century, but it was only after
the Second World War that they came to Hampshire.

An alternative route to Farnham goes through the
picturesque village of Selborne, which is sheltered
from the prevailing wind by a steep hill with a beech
copse on it. Selborne is best known as the home of the
Revd Gilbert White (1720–93), the famous naturalist.
As a young man he was a Fellow of Oriel College,
Oxford, but he spent the last forty years of his life
back in his native Selborne, where he enjoyed the

leisurely life of a gentleman while receiving the stipend of a benefice in Northamptonshire. Gilbert White House also houses the Oates Museum, dedicated to Captain Scott's self-sacrificing companion, Lawrence Oates and created by a previous owner of Gilbert White's house, a relation of Oates.

Those who make this detour can find their way back along the line of the A325 through Farnham's overspill at Wrecclesham, and so join the authentic route by the roundabout to the west of the town. Farnham merits some leisurely exploration, having preserved almost intact its eighteenth-century character. Off the High Street there are a number of attractive alleys; one of them, Lion and Lamb Yard, has been sensitively developed as an up-market shopping precinct.

Farnham stands at an ancient crossroads. Here three routes converge: the one from Winchester, the one from Portsmouth and the Harrow Way from Stonehenge. Extending eastwards from Farnham are the Pilgrims' Way, running along the Hog's Back, and routes to Aldershot and Godalming. The town is dominated by its castle, established in Norman times as a seat of the bishops of Winchester, a tradition which ended when the new diocese of Guildford was carved out of the see of Winchester in 1927. Farnham Castle was already established by the reign of Henry II, so it could well have provided the king with his first night's lodging after Winchester.

The castle's most memorable days were during the

Farnham Castle

Civil War, when it was first a Parliamentary and then a Royalist stronghold, at different times being besieged by both sides. In recent years it has been used commercially as a centre for briefing and debriefing mostly business people working abroad, especially in Third World countries. Before that it was a regular venue for selection conferences for candidates for the Anglican ordained ministry. A familiar prayer from The Book of Common Prayer may therefore be appropriate here:

✠

Almighty God, who alone workest great marvels,
send down upon our bishops and clergy
and all congregations committed to their charge
the healthful spirit of thy grace;
and that they may truly please thee,
pour upon them the continual dew of thy blessing.
Grant this, O Lord,
for the honour of our advocate and mediator,
Jesus Christ our Lord.
Amen.

Fourth Day
Farnham to Guildford (ten miles)

From Farnham to Canterbury the Pilgrims' Way is much easier to follow than it is in its progress through east Hampshire, since it largely coincides with the North Downs Way, which is clearly marked with its acorn sign throughout its length. There are certain points where it deviates from the traditional route of the Pilgrims' Way, but in general it provides a clear trail for the pilgrim who is not over-scrupulous about which route to follow.

The North Downs Way leaves Farnham in a south-easterly direction, away from the tangle of main roads, and within a couple of miles it passes Moor Park. This gentleman's country seat was the home of Sir William Temple on his retirement from serving as Charles II's ambassador in the Netherlands. Equally distinguished was his wife Dorothy, better known under her maiden name, Osborne. Her letters give a vivid picture of the life of the well-to-do in the countryside at the end of the seventeenth century. In the spacious hall of the house hang portraits by Lely of Sir William and his lady. One of the couple's protégés was Jonathan Swift, the acerbic Irish author of *Gulliver's Travels*, who went on to become

Dean of Dublin. It was in Moor Park that he had his infatuation with a young woman whom he referred to as Stella.

A hundred years later Farnham's best-remembered son, William Cobbett, wrote with great affection about the house and its gardens: 'I have never seen anything of the gardening kind so beautiful in the course of my life,' he wrote. Cobbett's enthusiasm is all the more remarkable since Moor Park stands on the fringe of those sandy tracts of Surrey which he so deplored as unprofitable soil.

Beyond Moor Park the acorned route zig-zags its way past Runfold, with its sandpits, to the southern flank of the Hog's Back. Those who care to negotiate the maze of lanes and paths that skirt the smart homes of west Surrey may go via Waverley. Of the great medieval Cistercian abbey little remains except one large east window-frame that gives an idea of the scale of the place. After the Dissolution of the Monasteries the abbey soon found other uses. As was often the case, the religious house became a gentleman's country seat. Here the wheel has come full circle, for Waverley Abbey House is now a conference centre run by a Christian Charity, opened in 1987 by Lord Tonypandy, former speaker of the House of Commons.

The A31 now climbs the Hog's Back on its north flank, so that the Pilgrims' Way, which runs along a lane to the south, is out of earshot of the traffic. It goes through Seale to Puttenham, both attractive and unspoilt villages. One curious feature of Puttenham Church is that the corbels on the four pillars of the north aisle rise up towards the east. Beyond Puttenham the Way crosses the B3000 and goes on to the greensand ridge that runs parallel to the chalk of the North Downs a couple of miles to the south. The Greensand Way is now marked as a long-distance walk running well into Kent. For the walker the great advantage of the greensand over chalk is that it dries out quickly. Even so, the traditional route of the Pilgrims' Way follows the chalk for most of the miles to Canterbury.

The North Downs Way is clearly marked as it leads over the A3 to the village of Compton. Noted for the two-storey sanctuary of its church, Compton is also the setting for the Watts Gallery, a gift to the village from the pre-Raphaelite artist George Watts and his wife. He is best known for his painting *The Light of the World* in St Paul's Cathedral. His last painting, *Destiny*, is in the collection at Compton.

Leaving Compton and heading towards Guildford, the route crosses Loseley Park, which belongs to the More-Molyneux family and well known for its superior brand of ice-cream. The approach to the River Wey is by the ruins of St Catherine's Priory a mile to the south of Guildford. From there a track leads down by a small stream to the water's edge. Just beyond the bridge over the railway is a Pilgrim Cottage with a mosaic of St Christopher carrying the infant Jesus across the river. For pilgrims today a

Guildford: A footbridge over the River Wey

sturdy foot-bridge takes them clear of the water, and the track runs on due east.

At this point the pilgrim may decide to call it a day and go into Guildford. Despite some modern development, this leading Surrey borough has kept much of its historic appearance, with the distinctive clock hanging out over the slope of the High Street. William Cobbett considered it 'the prettiest, the most agreeable and most happy-looking' town that he had ever seen. In a palace long since vanished Henry II often stayed here, and he created a park at Guildown where he hunted. Otherwise there is nothing that links Guildford with the Pilgrims' Way, which bypasses the town to the south.

Outstanding among Guildford's older buildings is Abbot's Hospital at the top of the High Street. It was founded by George Abbot, who served as Archbishop of Canterbury from 1611 to 1633. He was the son of a poor Guildford cloth-maker, but his two godparents were men of substance and saw him through school and Oxford. He went on to become vice-chancellor of his university before reaching the crown of his career. The old grammar school where his education began is still there, as are the remains of a medieval castle.

But a visitor to Guildford today should cross the river to discover its modern claims to fame. What was once the Battersea Polytechnic has established itself on the slopes of Stag Hill as the University of Surrey. It is not the only connection between the two places. On the crest of the hill stands Guildford Cathedral, the work of Edward Maufe, who also designed Battersea Power Station! Wags have often joked that it is difficult to distinguish between 'Guildford Power Station' and 'Battersea Cathedral'.

The interior of the cathedral is beautifully spacious and full of light. One detail that is worth noting is the engraved glass screen near the west door, the work of John Hutton. It shows a riot of angels trumpeting the Holy Spirit, to whom the Cathedral is dedicated. Another prayer from the 1662 Prayer Book is thus a proper conclusion to this part of the pilgrimage:

O Lord, who hast taught us that all our doings
without charity are nothing worth,
send thy Holy Spirit and pour into our hearts
that most excellent gift of charity,
the very bond of peace and all virtues,
without which whosoever liveth is counted dead
before thee.
Grant this for thine only Son Jesus Christ's sake.
Amen.

Fifth Day
Guildford to Dorking (thirteen miles)

The walk from Guildford to Dorking is the longest day's journey proposed in this book. It is also one of the most rewarding walks, rising to the height of St Martha's, with its splendid panorama, down through the pretty village of Shere, along the River Tillingbourne through Gomshall and Abinger Hammer, and from there up on to the North Downs and across Ranmore Common. By Ranmore Church the Pilgrims' Way is abandoned in favour of the gentle descent down into Dorking.

A mile south of Guildford on the Horsham road, the Pilgrims' Way crosses near a good pub named 'The Seahorse'. From there the route leads up through the Chantry estate and, steadily rising, reaches open country. It crosses a lane by an old stone that marks the Guildford borough boundary, and from the car-park there it climbs in a sandy swathe the final half mile to the crest. There stands St Martha's Church, sensitively restored in 1848 to its Norman simplicity. In the car-park is a notice-board which says when the church is open.

Open or not, its setting is breath-taking: to the north, one can see Newlands Corner and the line of the North Downs stretching away to the east; to the south there is a panorama with the South Downs as the backdrop. Beyond St Martha's, the North Downs Way turns north to strike directly across to the chalk. Pilgrims should continue to head east down a well-marked path that, after a couple of miles, crosses the main road between Albury and Shere, and then skirts the edge of Albury Park, the Surrey seat of the Dukes of Northumberland.

As a notice warns, the church on the right is private. It was built as the cathedral of the Catholic and Apostolic Church by a banker called Drummond, but the building was subsequently replaced by

Abinger Hammer: The Clock

the huge church in Bloomsbury that belongs to the same denomination. Also known as the Irvingites (a Scottish minister named Edward Irving [1793–1834] was one of the founders of the movement), the Catholic and Apostolic Church anticipated the Pentecostal ministries of our own days. At its height in the 1920s it had some eighty congregations in the United Kingdom, as well as others across the English-speaking world and in northern Europe.

The Pilgrims' Way follows the course of the

Tillingbourne, with its watercress beds, for a couple of miles through a string of villages. Beyond the green at Abinger Hammer it strikes diagonally up towards the crest of the North Downs in the woods to the west of Ranmore Common.

By Ranmore Church the traditional Way enters the Denbies estate, now the most extensive vineyard in England. Weary walkers may decide to head down the coach-drive that leads to Dorking for their evening's recreation and their night's rest. What distinguishes Dorking from other Surrey towns is its musical tradition. The Leith Hill music festival was initiated here under the baton of Ralph Vaughan Williams, and has continued to be the highlight of the town's cultural year, with the recently refurbished Dorking Halls as its base. So a prayer for St Cecilia's Day, the patron saint of music, makes a fitting conclusion to this long day's pilgrimage:

✠

Almighty God,
ruler of the heavenly spheres whose music we cannot hear,
open our ears to enjoy and our fingers to make
the music which knits up the sleeve of care
so that we may sing in our hearts
and prepare for the melody of heaven.
Amen.

Sixth Day
Dorking to Reigate (seven miles)

The previous day's walk was the longest; this one is the shortest. By road Dorking and Reigate are barely five miles apart; with a lift by public transport to rejoin the Pilgrims' Way where it crosses the River Mole, the day's walk is a couple of miles longer. The Way follows the curve of the downs up to Pebblecombe, and then climbs to the ridge and comes back down into Reigate. Any walker who wants to go a little further could go straight on to Merstham, but accommodation is more difficult to find there.

From Dorking Station a train to Box Hill or a bus to Burford Bridge would cut out the tedious walk along the busy A24 dual carriageway. Just before the bridge a track leads down through shrubbery to the stepping-stones across the river. These hexagonal blocks of concrete can be wet and slippery, so care should be taken in using them. Once the river has been crossed, the path is straightfoward enough to follow along the foot of Box Hill, but it only comes out into the open as it nears the first of the chalk-pits that mark this stretch of the downs. It is many years since they were worked, and the old workmen's cottages have been prettified. Close below the path runs the railway – one of the oldest in the country, built in the 1840s to link the Channel ports with Aldershot.

The route runs straight on until, above Betchworth Station, for half a mile it coincides with the main road that leads up to Pebblecombe. Where the road turns directly into its steep ascent, the North Downs Way is clearly marked as it heads off to climb the scarp more gently and to emerge on the top of the downs on the fringe of Walton Heath. It is also possible to keep to a path that maintains its contour at the foot of the scarp. (At the bottom of Colley Hill, where it meets the recommended route, this path is confusingly signed by the National Trust as 'The Pilgrims' Way'.)

The climb to the ridge is very worthwhile, even though the path at that point is very near to the M25,

Box Hill: Stepping Stones

for after crossing Walton Heath, the Way reaches an open half-mile of downland that offers rewarding views. Due south is a great sweep of the Weald, with planes going in and out of Gatwick Airport; on the horizon stands the hump of Chanctonbury Ring.

The Way passes a grand brick water-tower, and before the beech-woods close in it reaches a little rotunda built to contain a drinking fountain. The ceiling of the dome is a mosaic of the signs of the zodiac, and nearby is a plaque recording that this beauty spot was given to the nation in 1909.

From this point the Way runs down a great chalk gash in the side of the hill carved by the countless feet that have trodden this path over the centuries. As a metalled road it runs down the better part of a mile into Reigate, ending in a short stretch called Slipshoe Street. The name invites the assumption that here footsore pilgrims took off their boots before entering the 'Red Cross' or one of the other inns of Reigate.

A few years ago the 'Red Cross' reached the national news when its new owners dropped the name in favour of the generic name of their public-house chain. The Reigate Society protested loudly, but the old name was not restored. However, a painted red cross still dominates the inn's sign.

The name 'Reigate' has long puzzled etymologists. The preferred explanation is that it means 'the gap where the roe-deer sported'. In fact the name is first found only in the mid 1170s, a few years after Becket's murder. The Domesday Book refers only to 'Churchfelle', a settlement around the old parish church of St Mary's, half a mile to the east of the town centre.

The heart of Reigate lies in the lee of its castle, which Henry II had given to his bastard brother, Earl Fitzwarren. Reigate lies exactly half-way between Winchester and Canterbury, and so it would have been the obvious place for the penitent king to stay at the mid-point of his journey. It is therefore reasonable to think that the community growing up under the castle mound might have been given the name Reigate because it was 'the place where the king passed through' ('rei' is a recognisable variant of 'king', while 'gate' sometimes meant 'street', as one can still see from the street names in York). So the name Reigate may provide us with our surest indication that the Pilgrims' Way did indeed come into being following the route that the king took.

For Reigate, here is an acrostic prayer:

✠

Reign in our hearts, Lord,
Each step of the way
Inspiring our pilgrimage;
Guard us from glumness,
Assuage our restlessness,
Teach us to trust you
Every day. Amen.

Seventh Day
Reigate to Westerham (eleven miles)

This hard day's walk involves climbing up to the crest of the downs three times: up Reigate Hill at the beginning; up the ridge beyond Merstham three miles further on; and up Botley Hill above Titsey near the end of the journey, to go round a private park.

The suspension bridge at the top of Reigate Hill carries the Pilgrims' Way across the A217 and into Gatton Park. That too was private until the Second World War. It was the home of Sir Jeremiah Colman, the mustard manufacturer, who held magnificent firework displays, reflected in the lake here, to commemorate the silver jubilee of George V and the coronation of George VI. Until the Great Reform Act of 1832 Gatton was notorious as one of the 'rotten boroughs' that returned members to parliament despite having very small numbers of electors.

Beyond Gatton the Pilgrims' Way crosses the M25 by a new foot-bridge that leads to Merstham Church. One hint of the Way's authenticity is that this living is in the gift of the Archbishop of Canterbury. The next parish church, St Peter and St Paul Chaldon, half a mile north of the crest along which the Way runs, is well worth a visit by passing pilgrims. Its inside west

Chaldon Church: Doom painting

wall is covered with a medieval 'doom' painting. Layers of whitewash were removed in the 1920s, revealing a stark and vivid picture.

Its uncrowded top half depicts a few good souls being helped by angels up steep ladders into heaven. Its crowded lower half portrays men and women committing the seven deadly sins and, just below them, the cronies of hell are torturing their victims with gusto. Altogether, the painting invites the pilgrim, of whatever century, to a very scrupulous examination of conscience.

The route continues along the top of the downs, a switchback stretch as far as the A22 (the London—Eastbourne road). Beyond there the recognized trail descends once more to the foot of the scarp, only a field's width above the roar of the M25. A couple of foot-bridges across it lead enticingly to Oxted, but dogged pilgrims continue over the tunnel-mouth of the railway and on across chalk quarries.

North of Limpsfield they encounter their next obstacle – Titsey Park, for over 400 years the home of the Leverson-Gower family (the Dukes of Sutherland). Even now the route across the Park is open to the public only on a couple of days a year, when the house can be visited. Past Titsey Church the Titsey Foundation sign marks Pilgrims' Lane which leads to the Kent county boundary, and at that point a hard-pressed pilgrim may be very content to walk down into Westerham for a well-earned night's rest.

Westerham's most famous son is General Wolfe,

the young conqueror of Quebec city, and his statue dominates the centre of the small town. A couple of miles to the south lies Chartwell, for many years the home of Sir Winston Churchill, who also served as an imperial officer in his younger days, in India and then in Africa.

With these soldiers in mind, the 'military' prayer of St Ignatius Loyala of the Society of Jesus may not be out of place:

✠

Teach me, O Lord, to give and not to count the cost,
To fight, and not to heed the wounds,
To toil and not to seek for rest,
To labour, and not to ask for any reward
Save that of knowing that I do thy will.
Amen.

Eighth Day
Westerham to Wrotham (ten miles)

Several roads going from Westerham towards the downs cross the well-marked Pilgrims' Way. It is easy to walk eastwards along it past the villages of Brasted and Sundridge in the valley, and the motor-way is only just in earshot.

Visible through the trees at the east end of Brasted is Brasted Place, a handsome eighteenth-century mansion. Between 1952 and 1974 it served as a place of education for would-be Anglican ordinands who lacked the necessary academic qualifications to go straight to a 'normal' theological college. One of its innovative virtues was that it drew students from different traditions of churchmanship, so they had a 'deep-end' experience of the need for tolerance. For pilgrims who see themselves as pacing out the boundaries of belief, Brasted Place may well have a lesson to teach. Nowadays many candidates for ministry in the Church of England do their training in part-time schemes arranged by their dioceses, and so they often find themselves rubbing shoulders with those from traditions different from their own.

After passing Sundridge, the pilgrim is suddenly confronted by a notice saying 'Private'. This is the Chevening estate, which serves as a country home for the Foreign Secretary of the day, just as Chequers serves the Prime Minister.

Here the maps show the North Downs Way clambering to the ridge and then back down again past Fort Halstead. It is much shorter to circumvent the Chevening estate to the south, and then to rejoin Pilgrims' Lane just where the downs give way to the Darent valley.

That stretch of the lane leads to a chalk-pit, but the path continues on the right, only to peter out in a flight of steps. At the end of these the pilgrim should cross the A228 and immediately use the road-bridge to go over the M25. Beyond that the road sign says seductively, 'Pilgrims' Way West', but to avoid a miserable mile-long walk down the busy, narrow road into Otford, the pilgrim should look out on the right for the familiar acorn sign that offers a pedestrian approach to the river crossing.

Otford is an ancient village clustered round a green, with the remains of a medieval palace. The Church of St Bartholomew to one side of the green was one of the first churches in England to have a female vicar, although the nearby village of Wrotham had a female priest-in-charge two years earlier. Another historical landmark in Otford is the row of British Legion cottages, with their typically Kentish tile-hanging. They were built after the First World War to honour Lloyd George's promise of half an acre and a cow to the surviving soldiers. There was an unspoken belief that the offer of decent housing would make the war veterans more content and hence less likely to embrace communism, as their erstwhile Russian allies and many of their defeated German foes had done. The centrepiece of this politically inspired housing is the British Legion Village at Barming near Maidstone.

Eastwards out of Otford the Pilgrims' Way is easy to follow as it runs through Kemsing. I have a less-than-fond memory of this village! During our National Service training in Aldershot many years ago, a friend and I spent a long weekend of leave walking to Canterbury. We went all the way from Reigate to Kemsing in a single day. To our relief, quite late in the evening we reached Kemsing's Youth Hostel and readily paid five shillings each to join the organization. What we had not clearly understood was that every Youth Hosteller would be allocated a chore, and ours was to tidy up once everybody else had left after breakfast!

A mile short of Wrotham the metalled lane takes a sharp right turn, but a byway (which can be very muddy) goes on to the hillside village, where the pilgrim should be able to lodge for the night. Despite being entrapped by converging motorways and overshadowed by a forest of television relay masts, Wrotham preserves intact its timeless village character and is a welcome oasis.

The Diocese of Rochester's pilgrim prayer makes an appropriate end to this day of walking across its territory:

✠

Lord God, we thank you for calling us
into the company of those who trust in Jesus Christ
and seek to follow him.
Through your Holy Spirit
Lead us to journey deeper into the mystery of your love,
to be stronger in the bond of unity
and to be bolder in the ways of wisdom
and service to the world.
Give us the courage to invite many others
to join us together in pilgrimage,
for the glory of your holy name.
Amen.

Ninth Day
Wrotham to Aylesford (eight miles)

One of the puzzles for those who have tried to trace the exact route of the Pilgrims' Way from Winchester to Canterbury is where to cross the Medway. The modern North Downs Way makes its crossing in a fashion that is certainly not medieval. It follows the line of the downs on the west of the Medway where they curve northwards, crosses the river by the motorway bridge, and then comes back southwards on the east bank.

Aylesford is the natural crossing-point. There the river ceases to be tidal and an old foot-bridge spans it. What makes Aylesford particularly attractive for a pilgrim is its priory, locally known as 'The Friars'. All those plodding to Becket's shrine should make sure that they visit this beautiful place.

The walk from Wrotham to The Friars is pleasant enough to begin with, but the last two or three miles are a boring tramp through the riverside industrial area. Some pilgrims may instead prefer to get to The Friars by bus or train.

Those who are determined to walk will need to keep their eyes open as they leave Wrotham to find the Pilgrims' Way continuing eastwards from the roundabout where the A226 to Gravesend crosses the A20 from London. The route climbs the hill, and so the North Downs Way continues. A little-frequented lane offers an easy, downhill, one-mile walk to Trottiscliffe (pronounced 'Trosley'). Another mile along a byway brings the pilgrim to Trosley Court and the church that seems to be part of its domain. Here the direct route to Aylesford runs a mile through a wood to Ryarsh, and from there a further mile to Birling. So far so good.

Beyond Birling Church a footpath leads east and passes a marsh on its left. Just west of a roundabout the path reaches the Rochester–Tonbridge road (the A228) almost opposite a slip-road. Armed with a good map (Ordnance Survey 188 will do), pilgrims must then find their way through New Hythe, keeping the railway to the left and the M20 to the right until they converge by Aylesford Station. From there a well-signposted road leads past a cemetery to Aylesford Bridge.

The village hugs the right bank of the Medway, making its inhabitants (according to ancient local custom) Men and Maids of Kent, while those on the London side of the river are called Kentish Men and Maids.

'The Friars' is a half-mile walk downstream from the village. The Order of Friars Carmelite (to give them their correct title) founded the priory as their first English house in the year 1242, with Simon Stock as their prior. It evidently flourished for almost 300

Aylesford Priory: Pilgrims' Hall

years until the Dissolution of the Monasteries under Henry VIII. For just over 400 years the property was in private hands. In 1949 it was put on the market, and so the Friars Carmelite were able to buy back their old home. Since then it has served as a religious centre.

Much of the medieval building remains, and the Great Courtyard offers the newcomer an immediate sense of space and calm. Along most of one side is the Pilgrims' Hall, probably dating from the late thirteenth century – a hundred years after Becket's murder, and a hundred years before Chaucer's pilgrims. On the left of the Courtyard is the entrance to a passage to the cloisters, and there an unusual sight greets the visitor's eyes – an open-air shrine. Built to accommodate 3,000 worshippers, during the pilgrimage season it is often full. If there is rain, worship can take place in the adjacent Relic Chapel or in St Joseph's Chapel. Both have lovely modern glass, ceramics and sculptures.

Naturally, most of those who visit 'The Friars' are Roman Catholics, but those of other traditions are also made to feel welcome. The place has about it a sense of what might be called 'holy vulgarity'. Something similar is apparent in the Roman Catholic shrine in the Slipper Chapel at Walsingham, where the contrast with the gentility of the Church of England shrine is very stark.

The members of the monastic community at 'The Friars' wear their scapulars as a sign of their devotion

to Mary. One of their prayers expresses their commit-
ment well:

✠

Father, you called St Simon Stock to serve you
in the brotherhood of Our Lady of Mount Carmel,
under whose patronage he lived and worked.
Help us to honour the Mother of your Son
and to dedicate our lives to the work of redemption.

We come to you, St Simon Stock,
to ask for your help in our pilgrimage of faith.
Like you, we honour Mary, the Flower of Carmel,
and ask her patronage.
Obtain for us, through her intercession,
protection and guidance on our journey through life,
so that we may one day reach our home in heaven
and enjoy the blessings of God's peace.
Amen.

Tenth Day
Aylesford to Lenham (twelve miles)

Once the pilgrim is across the Medway, the pull of
Canterbury is almost tangible, and along these final
stretches of the Pilgrims' Way there are fewer diversions. Above Aylesford pilgrims rejoin the North
Downs Way by an ancient stone circle – a 'mini-
Stonehenge' – known as Kit's Coty House. Here, past
the village of Boxley, is the stretch of the route that
Roche first called 'the Pilgrims' Way' in his map of
1752. The Way is easy to follow through Detling and
beyond, at the foot of a scarp that is generally much
lower than it has been since mid-Surrey. The route
runs well above Maidstone and offers enticing views
of the Kent countryside, including a glimpse of Leeds
Castle through the trees.

All the way to Charing – a comfortable day and a
half's march – the Way is straightforward and pleasant, far enough above the M20 not to be spoilt by the
roar of traffic. With the coming of the high-speed
Eurolink railway, pilgrims face the prospect of an
occasional 'swoosh' as a train speeds by at 300 kilo-
metres per hour, but otherwise the trail of lane and
byway offers good walking.

The only habitations along this leg of the journey
are the hamlets of Thurnham and Broad Street and

the top of the village of Hollingbourne, whose street runs down the side of the hill to its church. Above Lenham there used to be a tuberculosis hospital, which has given place to a select residential development. A large cross cut into the chalk makes an unusual war memorial. At this point the pilgrim in search of a night's lodging can drop down into Lenham (which one can call either a small town or a large village), which has a variety of accommodation and places to eat, and the large and welcoming Church of St Mary.

For all that the Pilgrim's Way is a Christian track, any sensitive pilgrim should be glad sometimes to use prayers from other traditions. One of the simplest and most moving was written by a contemporary of Francis of Assisi, the Persian Sufi mystic known as the Mevlana:

Come, come, whoever you are, come to the Lord of Life.

Eleventh Day
Lenham to Boughton Aleph (ten miles) or Wye (twelve miles)

The next day's stint picks up the Pilgrims' Way as it goes on to Charing, which invites a saunter down its winding main street. On the left of a side-road are the ruins of a medieval palace, now incorporated into some farm buildings. The road leads on to the Church of St Peter and St Paul.

On from Charing, the Way crosses the main road to Canterbury and continues as a metalled lane. Later it turns into a byway which affords pleasant walking through an extended hazel coppice. The route then meets its final obstacle, Eastwell Park, whose mansion is now a five-star luxury hotel – hardly suitable for pilgrims! It would probably be best to skirt around the park rather than try to cross it.

South of the park the public road leads to Boughton Leys, where a left fork goes on to Boughton Aleph. This village, round its large green, is authenticated as being on the Pilgrims' Way. Here the North Downs Way divides, one branch continuing along the line of the hills as far as Folkestone, the other leading to Canterbury. Anyone who is not too foot-sore may decide to walk another couple of miles along the seabound branch to Wye, just over the River

Charing: Old Palace ruins and Church Tower

Stour. As well as being the home of the Agricultural College of London University, Wye has a number of interesting buildings, including an attractive medieval gatehouse, and offers a range of accommodation for the pilgrim.

In Charing Church visitors may still find this prayer from the Sudan:

Come everyone and beg God
To give life to mankind.
Come everyone and receive life
from God.
Rain mixed with sunbeams will give us life.

Twelfth Day
Boughton Aleph or Wye to Canterbury (thirteen miles)

The final day's walk keeps to the left bank of the Stour, with acorn symbols to mark the route as it winds its way towards Canterbury. In due course it reaches Chilham. With its black-and-white houses round an open square, it is one of the most beautiful villages of Kent. A mile further on, straddling the Stour, is Chartham. It makes no such claim, but it has an honest, workaday charm. From there the Pilgrims' Way climbs up once more and, going around some orchards, leads to Harbledown, where it joins the route that Chaucer's pilgrims took as they ambled their way down Watling Street.

Because of the folding of the low hills, it is not until Harbledown that the pilgrim gets a first sight of Canterbury Cathedral, with its great bell-tower dominating the landscape. *Ave mater Angliae!* ('Hail, mother of England!') is the city's motto, and even pilgrims who have walked all the way from the ancient capital of Winchester may feel the urge to say it out loud.

Having joined the route from London, the Pilgrims' Way enters Canterbury not by the Southgate but by the Westgate. Among the Victorian villas on the approach road is the charming Aucher House, built in about 1850 to house clergy widows. At the end of this road stands the Church of St Dunstan in the West, still a quarter of a mile short of the Westgate, but effectively the doorkeeper for the old city.

Saint Dunstan (who died in 988) was the outstanding archbishop of the Saxon period. He was born near Glastonbury and was educated by the Benedictine monks there. Legend says that he tweaked the devil's nose with his smith's tongs. History records that he founded many new Benedictine monasteries across southern England and East Anglia; that he devised and at Bath Abbey used the form of coronation service that has survived almost unaltered into our own times; and that he assumed the primacy of Canterbury. To celebrate the one thousandth anniversary of his death, a pilgrimage from Glastonbury to Canterbury was held in 1988, arriving on his feast day, 19 May. That day the mayor of the city came out to greet some 500 pilgrims, including a valiant group who had done the journey largely on foot.

Canterbury Cathedral – in the eyes of many the loveliest cathedral in England – is rightly proud of its many treasures, from medieval stained glass to the chapel at the far east end established by Dean de Waal to commemorate the martyrs of the twentieth century. Those who reach the Cathedral after all the effort of a pilgrimage will want to explore at their leisure all that it has to offer the 1.7 million visitors who come to it year by year.

Canterbury Cathedral from the ruins of St Augustine's Abbey

In 1997, to mark the fourteen hundredth anniversary of the coming of St Augustine to Canterbury, English Heritage opened a new museum in the grounds of St Augustine's Abbey. Medieval pilgrims came to this city to pay homage at the shrine of St Thomas Becket. Nowadays our historical perspective has broadened to take in Canterbury as a whole. We start from its Roman origins, preserved in St Martin's Church; in the abbey walls we see it as it was in

Saxon times; in the Cathedral itself we trace the centuries after the Norman Conquest, which produced St Anselm as well as Becket; and through the city as a whole, scarred as it was by bombing during the Second World War, we find in miniature all of England and all of its history. *Ave mater Angliae!*

We can conclude with a prayer written by another St Thomas – Thomas More – who, when he lived in Canterbury, worshipped at St Dunstan's Church, where he is still honoured:

✠

Glorious God, give me grace to amend my life,
and give me, good Lord,
an humble, lowly, quiet, peaceable, patient,
charitable, kind, tender and pitiful mind,
and with all my works, words and thoughts,
to have a taste of the Holy Blessed Spirit.
Give me, good Lord, a full faith,
a firm hope and a fervent charity,
and help me to love thee above myself.
These things, good Lord, that I pray for
give me grace to labour for.
Amen.